STARTUP SAVVY

40 DAY *Survive* to **FIVE**

CAMPAIGN

WORKBOOK

www.intrepidbizstrategies.com | Copyrighted Material

No part of this book may be reproduced, stored in a retrieval system or transmitted in any form or by any means without the prior written permission of the publishers, except by a reviewer who may quote brief passages in a review to be printed in a newspaper, magazine or journal.

STARTUP SAVVY: 40-Day Survive to Five Campaign Workbook

Copyright © 2015 Aundrea Y. Wilcox

All rights reserved.

ISBN-13: 978-1508880448

ISBN-10: 1508880441

Herein, I have developed a series of tactics that will re-energize you and breathe new life into your business, regardless of the type of business you operate and your place in the small business life cycle.

Instructions:

This workbook contains a 40-Day Survive to Five Campaign for increasing small business survival rates. Perform one tactical activity per day for 40 days straight, or just randomly select 6—10 items and perform the activities over the duration of one week or one month.

Ultimately, you don't just want to score points you want to survive and be wildly successful. Depending on your situation and resources, it may take you more than 40 days to complete this intense campaign. The point is to complete it. This series of tactics is not difficult to execute, but it does require using a steady snowball effect to produce a meaningful end result. The more you accomplish, the stronger you will become. Repeat the 40-day campaign as many times as you need to or any time your small business needs a shot in the arm, and remember that you will only win the game if you continue to play well.

DAY ONE

GET TO KNOW YOUR NEIGHBORS

If you don't know who your neighbors are, go visit them and introduce yourself. And while you are at it, visit City Hall and make an appointment to meet with your mayor and other city leaders. It will make all the difference in the world. You should know who they are and what they do and they should be as familiar with you. There is nothing worse than waiting until you actually have a problem and need their help, before you get to know your neighbors. It may surprise you to discover that they're not as bad as you might think, and they may actually want to see you be successful. Ask if they need help with anything, and be willing to roll up your sleeves if they do.

_____

_____

_____

_____

_____

_____

_____

_____

_____

_____

_____

DAY TWO

READ THE DAILY NEWS

I love reading the morning paper, even if I don't get to it until later in the day. If you work for the Chamber of Commerce, reading the paper is a minimal job requirement. How can you hope to be effective in the community if you don't know what's going on in it? In the business section you will usually find a calendar of events or notices about upcoming meetings and training opportunities, a listing or mention or new local startups, news reports, the most recent technological advances, stock performance, and business-related features and editorials.

_____

_____

_____

_____

_____

_____

_____

_____

_____

_____

DAY THREE

ATTEND YOUR OWN RIBBON-CUTTING

I have attended more ribbon-cuttings than I can count, but I promise, each one is important and worthwhile. You can organize your own ribbon-cutting or you can organize one in conjunction with your Chamber of Commerce. If you choose the latter, it may cost you something, but view it as an investment in the future success of your business.

_____

_____

_____

_____

_____

_____

_____

_____

_____

_____

DAY FOUR

GO PUBLIC

When something good happens in your business, get the word out immediately. If you are a startup and you haven't distributed a press release about your opening, do it today. If you are an existing business, you may be celebrating your anniversary this year, so let the community know that you have reached an important milestone.

_____
_____
_____
_____
_____
_____
_____
_____
_____
_____

DAY FIVE

CALL YOUR FAVORITE RADIO STATION

My friends say that I am somewhat of a news junkie. If I'm not watching the news on television or reading it in the paper, I'm listening to one of my favorite radio talk shows. Don't be afraid to call in to your favorite station and share your point of view, tell a joke, make an announcement, or invite the show hosts to drop in for a visit.

_____

_____

_____

_____

_____

_____

_____

_____

_____

DAY SIX

WRITE A LETTER TO THE EDITOR

How many times have you thought about writing a letter to the editor, but you decided to just drop it and let it go? Maybe, you were fearful of the consequences of public exposure? When you started pounding out the letter on your computer, you were probably upset about something that really touched close to your heart. I've got news for you. You don't have to be upset to write a letter to the editor.

_____

_____

_____

_____

_____

_____

_____

_____

_____

_____

DAY SEVEN

SEND A FRIEND REQUEST

I strongly support Facebook Fan Pages for businesses. If you have a business Fan Page, use it for prospecting for new customers. It's perfectly fine to continually coddle your loyal customers, but you must also acquire new customers at the same time in order to grow your business.

_____

_____

_____

_____

_____

_____

_____

_____

_____

DAY EIGHT

FLOAT A MARQUEE

When is the last time you saw a movie at the mall or local theater? I admit I actually partake in the pre-movie trivia and pay attention to the few entertaining commercials that are shown. The last time I saw a movie, I was happy to see that local merchants were finally starting to take advantage of big screen advertising.

_____

_____

_____

_____

_____

_____

_____

_____

_____

_____

DAY NINE

DROP A POSTCARD

You may be thinking that direct mail is outdated, but the truth is we still scan our junk mail before we junk it, don't we? That means keep you postcard mailers straightforward and simple. Leave enough space to write a handwritten note and pop it in the mail to some of your regulars or customers that you haven't seen in a while.

_____

_____

_____

_____

_____

_____

_____

_____

_____

DAY TEN

BE A BUY SPY

What has your competition been up to lately? Stop in for a visit—discreetly if possible. If you are a restaurant owner, you should know exactly how your customers are being served when they are not eating at your restaurant. How does your competitor's menu and pricing compare to yours? How is the service and atmosphere? Who are you surprised to see there?

_____

_____

_____

_____

_____

_____

_____

_____

_____

_____

DAY ELEVEN

SCHMOOZE 'EM

If you're trying to land a big new customer or account, you are going to have to make an investment in time and money. If you want them to buy a big ticket item from you, you are going to have to build a relationship, and that starts with running into them frequently at gatherings and events and striking up a real conversation. Don't worry about being blown off or ignored.

_____

_____

_____

_____

_____

_____

_____

_____

_____

_____

DAY TWELVE

JOIN YOUR CHAMBER

Joining the Chamber is not just for the big boys and girls—large manufacturers and major industry. Small businesses typically make up to eighty percent or more of membership. And contrary to popular beliefs, the Chamber is not just about socializing.

_____

_____

_____

_____

_____

_____

_____

_____

_____

_____

DAY THIRTEEN

CALL A FRIEND

Ask a friend who isn't intimately familiar with your business to come in and observe and work with you (not for you) for the day. They may point out some things to you that have gone right over your head or in one ear and out the other, because you have naturally developed a very narrow perspective of your business. You may even be pleasantly surprised when they suggest a new way to wrap items, or check out customers, or display products or services.

_____

_____

_____

_____

_____

_____

_____

_____

_____

_____

DAY FOURTEEN

READ A BOOK

It's never ever too late to learn. Take the day off or take a long lunch and read a book. Today's books are easy to read, not like back in the day when no one seemed to have a sense of humor. You can start with something as simple as one of the latest books by John Maxwell, a renowned author, speaker, consultant and businessman.

_____
_____
_____
_____
_____
_____
_____
_____
_____
_____

DAY FIFTEEN

THROW A PARTY

That's right! You heard me. Throw yourself a party—at your place of business. Invite existing customers and prospects to come in and check out your digs, meet new employees, learn more about your business, show off a new piece of equipment, or let them try something before they buy. But, before you invite everyone in, make sure your place is presentable.

_____

_____

_____

_____

_____

_____

_____

_____

_____

_____

DAY SIXTEEN

BE MYSTERIOUS

Run a mystery ad in the paper or a newsletter. For example: "The first ten new customers to call (999) 999-9999 and make an appointment (or place an order) receive a free gift today only." To be mysterious you have to leave a little to the imagination, so don't say too much.

_____

_____

_____

_____

_____

_____

_____

_____

_____

DAY SEVENTEEN

ROB A BANK

I mean your piggy bank, of course. Splurge on a never before used marketing tactic. How much would it cost you to have a sign flipper for a day? If it doesn't bring in more business, at least you'll be entertained. Use your spare change to buy online advertising, leftover radio or newspaper ads at a deep discount, or purchase an outdoor billboard sign in a rural area for $100 to $200 per month.

_____

_____

_____

_____

_____

_____

_____

_____

_____

_____

DAY EIGHTEEN

GIVE A LITTLE—SELL A LOT

Promotional gift items still work, especially if they are good quality and serve a purpose. Jump drives are extremely popular and handy these days, so they will be appreciated by most people. Also ear plugs for concert goers, eco-friendly items, subtly imprinted apparel, and items that are industry-specific are preferred.

_____

_____

_____

_____

_____

_____

_____

_____

_____

DAY NINETEEN

GET HAPPY!

If you haven't been to happy hour at the newest hot spot in town, give it try. You don't have to drink alcohol if you don't drink and no one is going to force you to consort with the unscrupulous crowd. If the thought of this makes you uncomfortable, don't go alone. Take a friend or business associate and stay for an hour to network and tell others about your business.

_____

_____

_____

_____

_____

_____

_____

_____

_____

_____

DAY TWENTY

GET LISTED

Make the time to register your business in as many free online and print directories as possible. Every link makes a difference and could lead to a possible sale. However, avoid using your personal email address and direct phone number in these listings. Instead, set up a general email account and toll-free number for this type of advertising, to help keep your inbox clear of junk mail.

_____

_____

_____

_____

_____

_____

_____

_____

_____

_____

_____

DAY TWENTY-ONE

GIVE A TALK

Most local civic groups and Rotary Clubs are always looking for speakers. Offer to speak, but don't plan to talk about your business directly. You need to talk about a subject that the group can relate to and will be interested in learning more about. If you are the owner of a hair salon, you can offer to speak on "Slowing Down Male and Female Balding." Who wouldn't be interested in that topic?

_____
_____
_____
_____
_____
_____
_____
_____
_____

DAY TWENTY-TWO

STRUT YOUR STUFF

Get outside your business and take a walk. Truly notice your surroundings. Do you have any new neighbors? Are there new signs in place? What do you notice about the traffic patterns and pedestrian routes? Are the sidewalks littered? Can passersby see into your business from the road? If so, what do they see?

_____

_____

_____

_____

_____

_____

_____

_____

_____

_____

DAY TWENTY-THREE

BLAST 'EM

Don't spam your customers without their prior permission. When you gather their email address, let them know what you plan to do with it. If you're going to be sending them updates, information, surveys, or advertisements, ask them if they agree to receive these types of emails and give them an option to unsubscribe at any time and with ease.

_____
_____
_____
_____
_____
_____
_____
_____
_____
_____

DAY TWENTY-FOUR

FIND THE CHEESE

Get in the picture-taking habit. You can use these pictures later in creative marketing campaigns. Take a picture of your storefront on a beautiful sunny day, or assemble a group of employees posed and smiling on a casual Friday, or snap a photo of you and your product looking your Sunday best (and doesn't' have to be on Sunday).

_____
_____
_____
_____
_____
_____
_____
_____
_____
_____

DAY TWENTY-FIVE

GET FADED

Sitting in a barber's chair for 30 minutes can be as effective as spending an entire morning on the golf course. In both cases, there's bound to be a lot of friendly chit-chat going on about all sorts of things. If you keep your eyes and ears open, you may pick up some new information about a competitor's future plans, what customers are saying about your business, or unmet customer needs.

_____
_____
_____
_____
_____
_____
_____
_____
_____
_____

DAY TWENTY-SIX

DROP IT IN THE CUP

There is an old saying that if you keep your fist tightly clenched, you can't receive God's gifts. This is true in business too. Loosen up your grip a little and give and more money will come your way. If giving to charity is new to you, do some research to determine what nonprofit organization you will support. Stay away from new organizations without a track record.

_____

_____

_____

_____

_____

_____

_____

_____

_____

_____

DAY TWENTY-SEVEN

SHOW OUT

Whenever there is an opportunity for you to showcase your products or services, do it. If you are a Chamber member, look for a designated table at Chamber events to distribute your literature. If there isn't a table available, ask for one. Attend trade shows that make sense for your business. Choose to sponsor high-profile events or activities, such as your Chamber's golf scramble.

_____
_____
_____
_____
_____
_____
_____
_____
_____
_____

DAY TWENTY-EIGHT

MAKE A QUALITY CALL

Are your customers really satisfied with your products or services? Do you have a system for collecting feedback from you customers about their experience with you? Even if you do, make a phone call or two, and ask how you're doing. They, more than likely, will be surprised that you have selected them for a quality control call.

_____

_____

_____

_____

_____

_____

_____

_____

_____

_____

DAY TWENTY-NINE

GET FOUND—ONLINE

I don't care what kind of business you have; one of the single most important assets to your business is your web presence. Don't blow it by publishing an amateur web site for your business—even if you don't think you will get many visitors initially. A good-looking, user-friendly web site can really set you apart from the competition.

_____
_____
_____
_____
_____
_____
_____
_____
_____
_____

DAY THIRTY

VOLUN-CHEER!

Giving back to your community isn't always achieved by giving money. Decide to give time to a good cause and get your hands dirty for a change. Really get in there and do something with a cheerful heart, whether that means making your community more beautiful by picking up trash in your downtown, participating in a Chamber membership drive, helping the merchants on your block organize a sidewalk sale, or becoming a board or council member.

_____

_____

_____

_____

_____

_____

_____

_____

_____

_____

DAY THIRTY-ONE

BE MORE THAN A SPECTATOR

When you notice a recognition event or celebration event going on outside, drop what you're doing for five minutes and go and check it out. It might be a ribbon-cutting at a new store at the mall, a tree planting, a veteran recognition ceremony, a ground-breaking event, or a press conference. These are all usually open to the public.

DAY THIRTY-TWO

REACH OUT TO ALIENS

My daughter hates it when I strike up a conversation with a stranger when we're out shopping or dining. Afterwards, I always tell her the same thing: "Meeting a stranger for the first time is good for the soul." You get the chance to reinvent yourself. A stranger knows nothing about you, so make sure you make the right first impression, whether that's about you, your community, or your business.

_____
_____
_____
_____
_____
_____
_____
_____
_____
_____

DAY THIRTY-THREE

STAY THE COURSE

Advertising is the best way to get the word out about your business when it is unknown to the public at large. If you want to measure whether it's working or not, reference a distinct phone number or email in the advertisement. When you get an email or the phone rings, you know the source of it. If you don't get anything at first, don't be too discouraged.

_____
_____
_____
_____
_____
_____
_____
_____
_____
_____

DAY THIRTY-FOUR

ASK A QUESTION—ONLY ONE

Break from the usual routine and conduct a poll (one question at a time) to take a very careful look at how your customers buy. You might ask when the last time they purchased something on the Internet was, or how often they buy online, or what they buy online. On average, how many times a week do they dine out, and on what night? The last time they shopped for clothes, how much did they spend?

_____

_____

_____

_____

_____

_____

_____

_____

_____

_____

DAY THIRTY-FIVE

JUMP-START THE BANDWAGON

Be the first one to suggest a sidewalk sale, downtown retail tour, block party, or service business expo. Don't wait for someone else to come up with all the great ideas to promote your business. If you start the movement, it might actually take off and bring new customers to your door.

_____

_____

_____

_____

_____

_____

_____

_____

_____

DAY THIRTY-SIX

DUST OFF

If you have time to sit on a beat-up old patio chair outside your business and watch cars and pedestrians go by, something is drastically wrong. This irritates me more than anything. Go inside and start dusting until you figure out what the problem is. If you're dusting off merchandise you forgot you had, you might be right on top of the problem.

_____

_____

_____

_____

_____

_____

_____

_____

_____

_____

DAY THIRTY-SEVEN

BE A MOVIE STAR

Video marketing is an effective way to create brand awareness and it's becoming increasingly popular among small businesses. If your product or service is complex, a well-done video demonstration might answer a lot of questions for your customer. Don't make your own movies, however. Seek some professional assistance or advice at the very least.

_____
_____
_____
_____
_____
_____
_____
_____
_____
_____

DAY THIRTY-EIGHT

SMELL THE ROSES

When you have a record sales day, buy yourself a red rose or release a red balloon filled with helium gas into the sky to celebrate. "You done good" and you should take the time to smell the roses. Immediately recognize your employees when they exceed their sales goals. Don't give them a chance to feel underappreciated.

_____
_____
_____
_____
_____
_____
_____
_____
_____
_____

DAY THIRTY-NINE

COUNT YOUR CUSTOMERS

Acknowledge the 50th or 100th customer on a given day. Let them know and they will tell a friend what happened to them: "Guess what? I was the 100th customer at Hair Benders today!" By the time the word gets out to the competition that they might be behind, some of their clientele will have already found your salon through word of mouth referrals.

_____
_____
_____
_____
_____
_____
_____
_____
_____
_____

DAY FORTY

SELF-ASSESS YOUR SUCCESS

In a crisis, having a written business plan is vital to your survival. Don't let another day come and go without developing one. Use a down sales day to revisit your strategy. Are sales on pace with last year or last season? Even if they are, things could change at any minute. If you are a startup, are you where you thought you would be in terms of your pro forma? If you are not on target, it is imperative that you come up with new strategies and action plans that will get you where you need to be.

_____

_____

_____

_____

_____

_____

_____

_____

_____

_____

_____

QUESTIONS?
COMMENTS?
CONTACT ME?

Aundrea Wilcox, President

Intrepid Business Strategies

1657B E Stone Dr. Ste. 196

Kingsport, TN 37660-4609

United States

Toll Free: (800) 560-1387

Fax: (800) 560-1387

Web Site: intrepidbizstrategies.com

Email: awilcox@intrepidbizstrategies.com

ABOUT THE AUTHOR

AUNDREA Y. WILCOX, Brenau University MBA, is currently the Senior Business Counselor of the Tennessee Small Business Development Center (TSBDC) at East Tennessee State University (ETSU) Kingsport Affiliate Office, and Executive Director of the Kingsport Office of Small Business Development & Entrepreneurship (KOSBE) at the Kingsport Area Chamber of Commerce, Tenn. She has provided technical assistance to over 1,200 individuals or businesses.

Previously, Aundrea provided expert testimony at a hearing of the Subcommittee on Contracting and Technology of the U.S. House of Representatives Committee on Small Business in Washington, D.C., and served as a session moderator on "Small Business Incubation" at the 55th Annual Tennessee Governor's Conference on Economic & Community Development.

In addition to being a full-time GrowthWheel Certified Business Advisor™, Aundrea has a long tradition of community service. She currently serves on the Holston Valley Medical Center Board of Directors as a member of the Executive Committee and Co-Chair of the Joint Quality Committee; she is a Board Member of the Holston Business Development Center Small Business Incubator; and a past member of the Board of Directors of the Northeast Tennessee Regional Entrepreneurial Accelerator. She is also a Selection Committee Member for the East Tennessee State University Roan Scholars Leadership Program.

Aundrea Y. Wilcox is also the author of *Superwoman Smarts: Activating Leadership and Substance*; and a contributing blogger on business and finance to The BOSS Network, which was recently named by Forbes.com as one of the Top 10 Entrepreneurial Websites for Women, and one of the Top 10 Best Career Sites for Women. She also recently collaborated with 25 consultants affiliated with the U.S. Small Business Development Center (SBDC) program, to help write a new book, The TriStart™ Matrix, which is designed to help entrepreneurs master three critical phases for a successful business start.

Originally from Michigan, Aundrea resides in Kingsport, Tennessee, with her husband Lonnie L. Salyer, a graduate of the University of Tennessee, who also earned his MBA from East Tennessee State University, and is currently a Global Procurement Manager of Energy at Eastman Chemical Company. Between them, they have two children—Barbara (21) and Cody (15).

Startup Savvy:
Strategies for Optimizing Small Business Survival and Success

ISBN-13: 978-1456097479
ISBN-10: 1456097474

Startup Savvy is jam-packed with relatable real-world entrepreneurial stories combined with rock solid advice to help you optimize your small business success!

Superwoman Smarts:
Activating Leadership & Substance

ISBN-13: 978-1503032866
ISBN-10: 1503032868

Superwoman Smarts is all about women, but smart men will read it too—for a better understanding of the women in their life. It's about learning from each other, embracing each other, accepting our differences and achieving success, and doing more with what we have.

www.ingramcontent.com/pod-product-compliance
Lightning Source LLC
Chambersburg PA
CBHW080616180526
45168CB00007B/2934